DATE DUE			

THOMAS NAST

THOMAS NAST

Cartoonist and Illustrator
by David Shirley

A Book Report Biography
FRANKLIN WATTS
A Division of Grolier Publishing
New York / London / Hong Kong / Sydney
    bury, Connecticut

Cover illustration by Michelle Regan,
from a cartoon © Corbis-Bettman

Photographs ©: Corbis-Bettman, 29, 41, 100; Linda Frydl/Library of
Congress, 77; New York Public Library, 2, 53, 58; Northwind, 20, 60, 64,
67; Thomas Nast Society, 16, 25, 93, 96, 97, 105, 109, 116. The remaining
images are in the public domain.

Visit Franklin Watts on the Internet at:
http://publishing.grolier.com

Library of Congress
Cataloging-in-Publication Data

Shirley, David, 1955–
    Thomas Nast : cartoonist and illustrator / David Shirley
        p. cm.—(A book report biography)
    Includes bibliographical references and index.
    Summary: Describes the life of the young German immigrant who
became a noted illustrator of magazines and a political cartoonist.
    ISBN 0-531-11372-8
    1. Nast, Thomas, 1840–1902—Juvenile literature. 2. Cartoonists—
United States—Biography—Juvenile literature. 3. Illustrators—United
States—Biography—Juvenile literature. [Nast, Thomas, 1840–1902. 2.
Cartoonists. 3. Illustrators.] I Title. II. Series.
    NC1429.N3S54   1998
    741.5'942—dc21
    [B]   97-8323
                                                                   CIP
                                                                   AC

CONTENTS

CHAPTER ONE

FOLLOWING FIRES

It was a cold, gray December morning in New York City. A fresh dusting of snow from the night before covered the broken sidewalks and cobble-stoned streets of Greenwich Village. Children throughout the neighborhood were awakened by the familiar sound of shovels scraping against stone, as landlords and local merchants struggled to clear the sidewalks of ice and snow before the business day began.

From his tiny bedroom on the second floor, ten-year-old Thomas Nast rubbed a handkerchief across the frozen windowpane so that he could see the scene below. For a moment, the sound of the shoveling had stopped. Two men with broad-brimmed hats and heavy wool overcoats stood shivering on the street corner surveying their work. Like the boy who was watching them, both men spoke with heavy German accents.

Across the street, a wooden-framed milk truck was parked idly, stocked full of bottles and crates. From his window, Thomas could see the frosty puffs of air rise from the nostrils of the two aging horses that were harnessed to the front of the wagon. At the back of the wagon, the milkman strained to squeeze one last crate onto the stack.

Suddenly, there was a racket from the other end of the street, and Thomas could hear the hooves of other horses clattering across the cobblestones. Even before he heard the sharp clanging of a cast-iron bell, Thomas knew instinctively that it was the local fire wagon.

The year was 1850, and the city of New York was growing rapidly. German Protestant families like the Nasts lived in the same crowded row houses with Jewish families from Eastern Europe and Catholic families from Ireland and Italy. Along the narrow streets of lower Manhattan, new cheap, wooden-framed houses were built side by side to accommodate the people who moved into the city each week. Because the homes were heated and illuminated by wood, gas, and kerosene, fires occurred almost every day.

One of the favorite pastimes of Thomas and his friends was to follow the horse-drawn trucks to the site of a fire. Thomas was a heavy boy with a wide face and short, stubby legs. Sometimes he lagged behind the other children on the way to school or had to take time out from a game because he was out of breath. But he enjoyed watching the firefighters more than anything else in his life. He was always the first one out the door when the fire truck rang its bell and the first child to arrive at the site of the fire.

The firemen wore enormous hats and boots and bright red shirts that matched the color of the fire engine. Each of them carried an ax in one hand and used their other arm to heave huge buckets of water over their shoulders effortlessly. Occasionally, the men would disappear into a building that had already been consumed by flames and smoke, and Thomas would hold his breath waiting for them to reappear. Somehow the men always managed to escape unharmed, and Thomas and his friends were amazed by the firemen's confidence and courage.

Whenever Thomas followed one of the trucks to a fire, he always carried with him a sketch pad and a pocketful of charcoal drawing pencils. He had been drawing pictures of fires and other scenes from the neighborhood since he was six years old, and the closet in his room was filled with illustrations of fires, snowstorms, and other dramatic scenes. Like many of the other families in the neighborhood, the Nast family was extremely poor, and they could scarcely afford the cost of pencils and pads for a school-age boy. Years earlier, however, a local merchant who sold art supplies had recognized Thomas's talent and agreed to give the boy all the drawing equipment he could use.

The huge redbrick building that housed the Big Six Fire Company stood only a few blocks down William Street from the Nasts' apartment. Thomas frequently stopped outside the fire station on his way home from school. He hoped to catch a glimpse of one of the men inside or to see the huge red fire engine as it rolled away from the building. Painted on the front of the fire truck was the head of a ferocious tiger. The big cat's sharp teeth were fully exposed, and its eyes glared wildly. Thomas drew picture after picture of the tiger in his sketchbooks.

More than anything else, the young boy longed to meet the Big Six Fire Company's chief, William Tweed. Like everyone else in the neighborhood, Thomas and his friends regarded Chief Tweed as the strongest and bravest of all the firemen. In the young boy's mind, William Tweed and the Big Six tiger were almost inseparable. Years later, an adult Thomas Nast would once again use his pencil to connect the two images—William Tweed and the tiger—in the minds of tens of thousands of New Yorkers. By that time, however, the two men would be rivals engaged in a bitter struggle for the leadership of the city, and Nast's drawings would have a devastating impact on the life and political career of his former hero.

CHAPTER TWO

Thomas Nast was born on September 27, 1840, in the tiny German town of Landau. A part of the German region known as Bavaria, Landau was located only a few miles north of the French province of Alsace. For several centuries, villages and towns in the two areas had frequently changed hands between Germany and France. In 1871, during the Franco-Prussian War, Alsace would once again be annexed by Germany. The province was returned to France in 1919 as a result of the Treaty of Versailles.

As a child, Thomas was exposed to the music, culture, and popular traditions of both countries. In his neighborhood, there was both a German Lutheran church and a small Catholic cathedral for citizens whose ancestors had come from France.

Although France and Germany were at peace

at the time of Thomas's birth, the two countries had often engaged in bitter military battles over the years. Because Landau was located so close to a country with which it was frequently at war, it was a fortified town. Landau was completely surrounded by a wide stone wall, and a stern, forbidding guardhouse stood at the center of town. Many of its citizens were employed as soldiers in the military.

Thomas's father was a local musician who made most of his living by playing trombone in the marching band of the Bavarian Ninth Regiment. At night and on weekends, Thomas's father also performed in the orchestra at the local theater. Occasionally, the older Nast would carry his son with him to a performance. Thomas was always amazed by the flamboyant gestures used by the actors on the stage and the bright, colorful sets behind the action.

While his father rehearsed during the day, Thomas stayed home with his mother and older sister. Two other brothers had died before Thomas was born. Each Sunday after church, the entire family took bouquets of flowers to the graveyard where the two boys were buried.

Like many other European countries during the 1840s, Germany was in a state of social and political instability. Recent changes in industry, transportation, and communication had caused many people to rethink their ideas about politics, religion, and work. The rapid growth of business and industry had made some people wealthy but left others very poor. As in the great industrial cities of England, France, and the United States, factory workers frequently labored long hours under desperate conditions for little pay.

In the midst of this confusion, various political movements and leaders competed for the chance to govern the nation. Political movements representing the wealthy promised continued prosperity, along with law, order, and political stability. Groups representing workers and the poor called for greater political freedom for the masses and public ownership and control of the factories.

A NEW HOME

Fearing that his country would soon be gripped by a violent revolution, Thomas's father decided that it would be safer to send his wife and children away from their homeland. In June 1846, he enlisted as a sailor on a French military ship and bought his family tickets on a boat to the United States. Along with his mother and sister, Thomas sadly left Landau. Together they traveled by carriage across the French countryside, stopping briefly to visit the spectacular cities of Strasbourg and Paris.

After a few weeks, the Nast family finally arrived in the port city of Le Havre. From there, they sailed to New York Harbor and the city of Manhattan, where they had decided to make their home. Onboard the American ship that carried him and his family to the United States, Thomas got his first chance to hear people speaking English, the language that he would speak for the rest of his life. He was immediately befriended by the ship's captain and his wife, and Thomas laughed out loud as he tried to imitate the strange words that they said to him.

Learning to speak English did not come easily to the six-year-old boy. The family settled in New York on William Street in a quiet, tree-lined neighborhood. Most of the families in the neighborhood were recent immigrants from other countries. Few of them had arrived as recently as the Nasts, however. Other children at school and on the streets frequently made fun of Thomas's heavy German accent and his failure to remember some English words.

Frustrated by his inability to communicate with his teachers and friends in his new language, Thomas began to draw pictures. He soon discovered that it was much easier to draw a picture of a scene or event than to try to describe it in words. In class, he often scribbled portraits of his classmates in his notebook while the teacher was delivering the lesson. Sometimes, this got him into trouble. But it soon became obvious to his teachers and his mother that the youngster had tremendous talent, and Thomas was encouraged to continue his drawings both during and after school. To show her support, Thomas's mother began to cover the walls of the family's apartment with his drawings.

In 1850, Thomas's father finally arrived from France. It had been almost four years since Thomas had last seen his father, and the two of them began to spend every available moment together. The elder Nast quickly found work performing in the orchestra at Burton's Theater, a small but popular stage on Chambers Street. Thomas frequently accompanied his father to the evening's performance, sitting in a special chair in the back of the orchestra pit.

At Burton's Theater, Thomas first saw the plays of William Shakespeare performed. Such plays as *Hamlet, Julius Caesar,* and *Macbeth* left a lasting impression on the young boy, and he would later borrow images and characters from these and other Shakespeare plays in his adult work as an illustrator.

Thomas's father also took his son with him to see a number of famous people who visited New York City during the early 1850s. When visiting dignitaries arrived in the city, they were some-

Nast sketched these portraits of his father,
Joseph, and his mother, Appolonia.

times honored with huge parades that marched across Wall Street, just a few blocks south of the Nasts' home. Thomas was most impressed by the military leaders he saw. A drawing he made of the Hungarian general Lajos Kossuth was framed by his teacher and hung on the classroom wall. Thomas also admired the Italian general Giuseppe Garibaldi. Nast saw Garibaldi on several occasions, and his sketch books were filled with drawings of the Italian patriot.

LEARNING HIS CRAFT

By the time Thomas was 13 years old, his parents had accepted the fact that their son was destined to become an artist. With their permission, he dropped out of school and began to take drawing lessons full-time. For a few months, he studied in the studio of Theodore Kaufmann, a German painter who specialized in historical scenes and portraits. After Kaufmann's studio was destroyed by a fire, Nast enrolled in the Academy of Design on Thirteenth Street. At the Academy, Nast met other talented young artists. With his new friends, he visited the city's great museums and art galleries, where he became familiar with the work of the great painters and etchers of Western art.

In 1855, Nast heard about a new magazine, *Leslie's Weekly,* that featured drawings of the people and events that made the news each week. Although he was only 15 years old at the time, Thomas's drawing skills had matured rapidly during the previous two years. He was confident that he could make a real contribution to the magazine if its publisher, Frank Leslie, would only give him the chance.

One day, Thomas piled a stack of his best drawings under his arms and marched uptown to the *Leslie's Weekly*'s office. To his surprise, he was admitted into the editorial room, where he soon found himself face-to-face with Frank Leslie. A friendly, generous man, Leslie was amused by the sight of the short, chubby teenager with his arms crammed full of sketchbooks. Leslie was also an astute judge of talent, and he was immediately impressed by the quality of Thomas's work.

"So you want to draw pictures for my paper?" asked the publisher in a stern, demanding voice. "Very well. Go down to Christopher Street next

"So you want to draw pictures for my paper?"

Sunday morning, where the people are boarding the ferry for the Elysian Fields [a resort area across the Hudson River in New Jersey], and make me a picture of the crowd just at the last call of 'All Aboard!' Do you understand?"

Nast knew immediately that it was a difficult assignment, even for an experienced newspaper illustrator. The port at Christopher Street was so crowded and the people moved so fast that it would be almost impossible to capture it in a drawing. But Nast also realized that this might be his only chance to work for *Leslie's Weekly*. He was determined to do a good job, whatever it took. "Yes, sir. All right," he said and rushed out the door before the amused publisher had a chance to change his mind. Leslie would later confide to a friend that he never expected Nast to be able to complete the task. He had given him the difficult assignment "merely for the purpose of bringing home to his youthful mind the absurdity of his application." What the publisher failed to realize was that the 15-year-old Nast had spent his childhood drawing speeding fire engines and parades.

By the time the passengers began boarding the ferry the next Sunday morning, Nast had already sketched the dock, the harbor, and the scenery behind it. By the end of the day, he had completed the scene, and the drawing was ready for Leslie when he arrived at work the next morning.

THE FIRST JOB

Leslie was so impressed with Nast's talent and enthusiasm that he hired him on the spot as a full-time illustrator for *Leslie's Weekly*. The young artist was thrilled to receive a salary of $4 per week and to get the chance to work with such noted illustrators as Frank Bellew, Fitz-James O'Brien, George Arnold, and Miles O'Reilly. The older men frequently teased their teenage coworker. They nicknamed him "Roly Poly" and made jokes about his lack of knowledge of politics and other social issues. In time, however, they grew to respect Thomas's talents and his commitment to his profession, and they accepted him as one of their peers.

While working at *Leslie's Weekly,* Nast got his first chance to take part in an important social crusade. Early in 1858, Frank Leslie learned that several of the city's leading milk suppliers were using diseased cows in their milking stables. Although many people had recently become sick,

This is the cover of the April 18, 1874, issue of Leslie's Illustrated Weekly. *In 1855, Frank Leslie gave 15-year-old Thomas Nast his first job as an illustrator.*

the companies would not acknowledge that the milk they provided was contaminated or take any responsibility for the growing epidemic. Leslie sent a team of reporters and artists to sneak into the stables and document the condition of the cows.

Leslie's Weekly's aggressive coverage of the "Swill Milk Scandal" exposed the guilty companies to both the public and city investigators and helped put an end to the epidemic. Nast's drawings of the dilapidated stables and diseased cattle played an important role in alerting the public to the problem.

Nast was grateful for everything he learned during his four years at *Leslie's Weekly*. Frank Leslie had given the ambitious young illustrator his first chance to draw for a major publication. The publisher had also shown the young artist the important role that a committed journalist could play in addressing social problems. Leslie proved to be less committed, however, to paying his employees. The magazine's payments to Nast and his fellow artists were frequently late, and sometimes writers and artists were not paid at all for a particular assignment.

By the beginning of 1859, Nast had developed a reputation as one of the best young illustrators in New York. Several of *Leslie's Weekly*'s rivals began to offer him drawing assignments, often offering him more money than he was currently making. Nast soon began to accept many of these assignments. During the early part of 1859, Nast's illustrations appeared at various times in the *Sunday Courier,* the *Comic Monthly,* and the *Yankee Notion.* By the end of the year, Nast was no longer submitting any of his work to *Leslie's Weekly.*

Nast's most significant contribution during 1859 was to a newly formed weekly newsmagazine called *Harper's Weekly.* The magazine's first issue appeared that March, featuring some of the leading writers and artists of the day. Nast's old friend and mentor from his drawing school days, Alfred Fredericks, was on *Harper's Weekly's* editorial board, and he quickly recruited his young protégé to draw for the magazine.

AN ENGAGEMENT

During the summer of 1859, Nast met and fell in love with an attractive young woman named Sarah Edwards. Sarah lived with her family in a spacious home at 745 Broadway. As a child, Thomas had rarely ventured into the wealthy part of the city where Sarah and her family lived. Now a celebrated young illustrator for some of the city's leading publications, he was a regular guest at the parties and other social events held at the Edwards home. Throughout the summer, the young couple were frequently seen together, walking in Central Park or dining in one of the fashionable restaurants near the Edwards home. By the end of the year, they had already announced their engagement.

AN ARTIST ABROAD

In the winter of 1860, Thomas Nast was only 19 years old and at the very beginning of his career as a political cartoonist. His drawings from the period are finely detailed, with heavy pencil strokes, and reveal an unusually vivid imagination for so young an artist. Nast's early drawings were still basically illustrations for someone else's stories, however. Even the best of them lack the bold humor and raw emotional impact that would later earn him the reputation as the most important political cartoonist of his age. He still needed to discover his own unique way to bring the people and events that he observed to life for his readers.

In spite of Nast's youth and inexperience, he had already begun to receive steady work from several popular papers and magazines in New York. On February 15, 1860, the recently formed *New York Illustrated News* sent Nast to London, England, to cover a boxing match between British fighter Thomas Sayers and American boxer John C. Heenan.

When Nast arrived in London in early March,

the forthcoming fight was the most widely dis-
cussed event of the day. The young illustrator
joined Heenan and his companions for a month-
long tour of England. The outdoor boxing match
was held on April 17, 1860. In front of an enormous crowd, the two bare-fisted boxers battled
each other for a remarkable 42 rounds. From the
perspective of Nast and the other Americans in
the crowd, Heenan was clearly in control for most
of the match. The American fighter repeatedly
pounded Sayers against the ropes, knocking the
English champion to the floor on several occasions. To the dismay of Nast and the other Americans at ringside, the match was judged to have
been a draw, and both Heenan and Sayers were
presented with a championship belt in a ceremony following the fight.

Back in the United States, the *New York
Illustrated News* devoted an entire special issue to
coverage of the championship fight. Nast's drawings of the event were featured throughout the
paper. At the center of the paper was an enormous
double-page illustration by the artist. In the
drawing, two shirtless men stand face to face in
the center of the ring, each with his fists raised
menacingly toward the other man's body. A large
crowd watches anxiously from behind the ring.

Following the fight, Nast suddenly found
himself penniless and stranded in London. For his
work covering the Heenan-Sayers fight, the young

*This Nast drawing of the Heenan-Sayers
fight appeared in the April 17, 1860, issue of*
New York Illustrated News.

illustrator had received a money order from the
New York Illustrated News. Unfortunately, the
money order could only be redeemed for cash after
he returned to the United States, and he had too
little money to purchase a ticket for a boat trip
back to New York. Fortunately, John Heenan had
remained in England after the title fight to take
part in a series of exhibition bouts with Sayers.

The American boxer graciously offered Nast a place to stay while he looked for work.

GARIBALDI

In the early spring of 1860, Nast heard the news that Italian general Giuseppe Garibaldi was preparing a full-scale military invasion to liberate his homeland from the Austrian Empire. In 1848 and 1849, the Italian patriot had led two failed campaigns against the Austrian forces that occupied much of Italy at the time. After a decade of exile from his country, Garibaldi returned to Italy in 1859. After major victories in northern Italy, he marched south, along with his thousand-man army of red-shirted rebels, to confront the Austrian forces in the Italian kingdoms of Naples and Sicily.

As a small child, Nast had been captivated by stories of Garibaldi's first Italian campaign. The young illustrator decided that he had to find a way to meet the great Italian general and witness the Italian revolution for himself. Within a few weeks, he had persuaded the editors at a small English newspaper, the *London News,* to send him to Italy to draw firsthand accounts of Garibaldi and the Italian revolution.

While the struggling paper agreed to publish the young artist's work, they could not afford to pay the costs of his transportation to and from Italy. Once again, John Heenan came to Nast's rescue, providing him with the money he needed to begin his journey.

Nast embarked for Italy on the first available boat across the Mediterranean Sea. After a brief layover in Genoa, on the Italian mainland, he caught up with Garibaldi's latest military expedition on the island of Sicily. After his arrival in the Sicilian capital, Palermo, the young illustrator finally met Garibaldi face to face and was immediately impressed by the simplicity of the Italian leader's manner and dress. For his part, Garibaldi admired Nast's youth and enthusiasm, and the two men talked together frequently.

In Palermo, Nast also gained his first exposure to the enormous costs of war. Only a few days before Nast's arrival in Palermo, Garibaldi's forces had reclaimed the city as part of a united Italy. At the center of the Sicilian capital, angry gangs used axes and clubs to dismantle the buildings that had housed the old government. Great fires consumed entire neighborhoods from one end of Palermo to the other. The burned corpses of soldiers and other citizens lay piled in alleyways and on street corners.

Along with the destruction, Nast also witnessed great excitement and joy among the liberated citizens. Garibaldi and his troops were welcomed as heroes as they marched and paraded on horseback throughout the city.

Nast recorded these scenes of suffering and celebration in his drawings for the *London News*. In one picture, a huge crowd of Sicilian soldiers raises their rifles and swords above their heads to greet Garibaldi and his red-shirted troops at the gate to the city.

From Palermo, Nast continued with the expedition to several cities on the Italian mainland. Again, Nast and his fellow travelers arrived a few days after Garibaldi's army had captured each city. When the expedition reached Messina, Nast and his new friends discovered that the defending army had surrendered without firing a shot. It was only a matter of time, the artist realized, until Garibaldi's troops would raise the Italian flag in every city and village throughout the country.

Before reaching Naples, Nast and the other members of the expedition finally caught up with Garibaldi's main forces, and the young artist got a firsthand view of the general's triumphant entry into the city. A huge mass of people had assembled to greet the liberating army. The large drawing of this event that Nast later submitted to the *New York Illustrated News* was his liveliest and most imaginative illustration to date. Throughout the picture, Garibaldi's soldiers struggle in vain to keep the crowd from collapsing into the Italian general's carriage.

HEADING HOME

In Naples, Nast finally decided to leave the expedition. In spite of the thrill of the military campaign, the ambitious young illustrator had begun to miss his life in New York. He wrote daily letters to his fiancée, Sarah Edwards, and the young cou-

Nast sketched this illustration of Italian patriot Giuseppe Garibaldi entering Naples in 1860.

ple decided to marry when he returned to America. "I guess I've got sketches enough," he had told an American acquaintance only a few days before.

"I guess I've got sketches enough."

The two men had recently witnessed a violent battle between Garibaldi's soldiers and the opposing forces in Capua. The Siege of Capua would be the last serious stand against Garibaldi's forces.

On November 3, 1860, Nast traveled north on horseback to Rome. In the Italian capital, he visited many of the most famous Roman ruins, including the Coliseum. A sketch that he made of the structure's crumbling walls would later appear in many of his most important cartoons. In Rome, Nast also visited several art galleries and museums where he studied the paintings of Michelangelo, Leonardo da Vinci, and other great Italian painters.

After a few days in Rome, Nast traveled north to France and Germany. Before returning to America, he had decided to visit Strasbourg and his childhood home in Landau. He traveled most of the way by carriage or on horseback, and the journey to northern Europe took almost three weeks. After his recent experiences in New York, London, and Rome, Strasbourg seemed tiny by comparison. The village of Landau was even smaller. The fortress's dark, austere guardhouse and the wide city walls had once frightened him as a child. Now the tiny German village made him marvel at the greater, more impressive sites and wonders he had seen in the 14 years since his family had left Germany for New York.

In Landau, the young artist was welcomed as a returning hero. Throughout Europe, people had been closely following Garibaldi's war for Italian unity and independence. When Nast's family and friends in Bavaria learned that he had recently been at the Italian general's side, they overwhelmed him with questions and praise. Several dinners and parties were held in his honor, and he joyfully took part in all the elaborate Christmas celebrations being held throughout the holiday season. From Landau, he journeyed to the town of Nabburg, where he visited his father's birthplace and even spent the night in the same hard, simple bed where his father had slept as a boy.

Back in London, Nast submitted his remaining drawings and sketches from the trip to the *London News.* The editors at the paper were so impressed by the young illustrator's work that they offered him a permanent position. After almost a year in Europe, however, Nast was eager to return home to Sarah Edwards and the rest of his friends in New York. He collected his remaining wages from the *London News* and booked a ticket for the American steamer, *Arabia,* which was scheduled to sail on January 19. The previous January, Nast had left New York as a rookie illustrator, nervous about embarking on his first foreign assignment. Now he was returning home as a seasoned political cartoonist who was beginning to develop a style of his own.

CHAPTER THREE

THE GREAT WAR

The *Arabia* sailed into Hudson Bay and the gray icy waters of New York Harbor on February 1, 1861. Almost a year had passed since the 19-year-old Nast had left New York for London to cover the Heenan-Sayers fight. During that brief time, the young artist had traveled throughout Europe, witnessing some of the most significant events and meeting some of the most influential people of his age.

Arriving back in New York, the young illustrator had little time to reflect on his rich experiences in Europe. For one thing, he was desperately in need of work. Years later as an old man, he would boast to his biographer Albert Paine that he had only a dollar and a half in his pocket as he stepped off of the *Arabia*'s gangplank and onto the frozen sidewalks of lower Manhattan. He realized sadly that his plans to marry Sarah Edwards and start a family would have to wait until he had enough money to support her. For the time being, the young artist's days and nights would be spent in his studio, drawing pictures of the leading people and events of the day.

Nast resumed his work for the *New York Illustrated News,* receiving the same modest salary for the same backbreaking workload and hectic schedule. But Nast had little time to complain. He was quickly making a name for himself as the most talented young newspaper illustrator in America. And there was never a shortage of colorful people or exciting events to occupy his imagination and his drawing pencils.

A NATION DIVIDED

The hardships faced by Nast seemed almost insignificant compared to the great regional conflict that had now begun to divide the country. The November 1860 election of Abraham Lincoln as president had sharpened old disagreements between Northern and Southern citizens and brought the young nation to the brink of war. In recent years, citizens in the South had begun to voice their disapproval of many federal laws and regulations. Southern leaders insisted that the individual states themselves—and not the federal government in Washington, D.C.—should make their own decisions about important issues, such as the European nations with whom they would trade raw materials and products. During his campaign, Lincoln opposed the efforts of individual states to defy federal rule and control their own destinies. He promised that, if he was elected, he would enforce the nation's laws and trade regulations, and bring everyone together into a single Union.

The biggest issue that divided the nation during this period was the practice of slavery. Americans and Europeans had been capturing the inhabitants of western Africa and forcing them into slavery for almost 250 years. During that period, millions of African men, women, and children had been brought across the Atlantic Ocean in chains and then sold on auction blocks as the property of anyone who could afford them. For generations, slaves were bought and sold in virtually every inhabited region of North and South America.

In recent years, however, many citizens had begun to speak out against slavery. England, once a leader in the slave trade, had outlawed the practice in 1807. Since that time, most Northern slaves had been given their freedom, and the practice gradually began to disappear in the region. The movement to ban slavery in the United States, known as the abolitionist movement, had also become more and more powerful during this period, and its leaders, the abolitionists, had become increasingly outspoken. This was unwelcome news for Southern farmers and plantation owners. The booming economy of the South was based primarily on cotton and tobacco farming, and most farmers depended for their profits on the free labor of slaves and the cheap labor of poor whites.

Many Southerners feared that the abolition of slavery would bankrupt the South's economy and badly weaken the region politically. They recognized that Lincoln's presidential victory was a victory for the abolitionist movement. On December 20, 1860—only a few weeks after Lincoln's election—South Carolina became the first state to secede from the Union. Secession meant that a state would no longer obey federal laws, pay federal taxes, provide troops for the military, or participate in national elections. During the next few weeks, six more states followed South Carolina's example and began to form the Confederacy. As the day of Lincoln's inauguration grew nearer, both Northern and Southern citizens looked to the capital to see how the new president would respond to the growing crisis.

Shortly after his return from Europe, Nast was assigned by the *New York Illustrated News* to cover the presidential inauguration ceremony in

Washington, D.C. During his travels, the young artist had eagerly read letters and newspaper articles about the election and the growing conflict between the North (the Union) and the South. Like Lincoln, Nast bitterly opposed both slavery and secession. For Nast, the newly elected president was a heroic figure and a symbol of national unity. As he had done with Garibaldi in Italy, the *News*'s illustrator decided to use his talent and his popularity to support Lincoln's cause.

Nast got his first glimpse of the thin, bearded president in New York City on February 19, 1861, when Lincoln made the first stop of his triumphant train ride to Washington, D.C., from his home in Springfield, Illinois. Like the rest of the nation, the thousands of people who gathered to greet the president at his stops in New York, Philadelphia, and Baltimore were divided in their opinions of him. While many cheered loudly wherever he went, others jeered and hissed, and arguments and fights sometimes erupted between opposing sides.

Newspapers and magazines across America were also at odds regarding their attitudes toward and depictions of the newly elected president. An illustration for the March 9, 1861, issue of *Vanity Fair* portrayed Lincoln as a coward, hiding from the angry crowds beneath a scotch cap and an oversized army coat. Nast, on the other hand, was one of Lincoln's most ardent supporters during the period. His drawings consistently depicted the new president as a strong, brave, soft-spoken leader.

Completing his tour of the Northeast, Lincoln finally arrived in Washington, D.C., where he delivered his acceptance speech on March 9, 1861. Everyone in attendance was aware of the threat of violence, and armed police and military guards were posted at every corner to protect the president and maintain order. Lincoln delivered a passionate plea for unity and peace. "We are not enemies, but friends," he told the crowd. "We must not be enemies. Though passion may have strained, it must not break our bonds of affection."

Three months later, on April 12, 1861, fighting began in earnest when General Beauregard commanded his Confederate troops to open fire on a group of Union replacement troops arriving at Fort Sumter, near Charleston, South Carolina. By this time, four more Southern states had left the Union. Three months later, the Civil War's first major battle was fought at Bull Run.

For the remainder of 1861, Nast's dramatic pencil drawings of Lincoln and the events of the war continued to appear on the pages of the *New York Illustrated News*. In New York, where Nast spent most of his time, Lincoln faced opposition on two sides. Many people opposed Lincoln's call for a strongly united nation and supported the South's attempt to remain independent. On the other side were the abolitionists, who felt that Lincoln was moving too slowly to end slavery and punish the South.

Both the abolitionists and the Southern sympathizers frequently held protests in the city, denouncing Lincoln and his policies. With his fierce loyalty to Lincoln, Nast depicted both sides as traitors to the Union cause in his illustrations for the *News,* while the president was always presented as a hero.

In the spring of 1862, Nast was suddenly fired by his employers at the *New York Illustrated News.* He had recently been given a generous raise (from $30 to $50 a week) and he may have become too expensive for the struggling newspaper. Possibly the strong, one-sided political opinions he expressed in his drawings may have been too controversial in a city as diverse as New York. Nast had little time to worry about his sudden joblessness or to ponder the reasons why the News had dismissed him, however. Several drawings that he had sent to the prestigious *Harper's Weekly* magazine were immediately accepted at a much higher fee than he was accustomed to making at the News. By the beginning of summer, publisher Fletcher Harper had hired Nast as a regular contributor at twice his former salary.

At *Harper's Weekly,* Nast would establish himself as the most admired political cartoonist and illustrator in the history of American journalism. At the *New York Illustrated News*, Nast's job had been to create illustrations to accompany written stories about current events and people. At *Harper's Weekly,* the young artist was encouraged to make pictures that stood on their own and told their own stories. Some of his larger drawings with the magazine covered two full pages. Most of Nast's illustrations for the News had been scribbled hurriedly in the crowded newspaper studio to meet the deadline for the next day's news. At *Harper's Weekly,* Nast was allowed to work in the comfort of his home studio at his own pace.

Under these improved conditions, Nast's talents suddenly began to bloom. His series of large, highly decorative Civil War pictures helped shape the attitudes of thousands of Americans toward the war. Many people either did not read or quickly forgot the content of the articles in the magazine. But the moving, dramatic images in Nast's pictures often stayed with them much longer.

Nast's sentimental war pictures would continue to comfort and inspire people during the remaining years of the war. His drawings in the summer of 1863, "Hero of Vicksburg" and "Unconditional Surrender," convinced many Americans that Union General Ulysses S. Grant was the mil-

Nast titled this amusing self-portrait "Thomas Nast: The Young Artist Rushing Along the Turnpike of Fame." By age 22, Nast was well-established as an illustrator and cartoonist.

itary savior who would finally end the war. In the Christmas issue of that same year, Nast depicted Lincoln as a great peacemaker, inviting the representatives of the Southern states to take their place at the Union table.

By this time, Lincoln himself had become a close follower of Nast's work for *Harper's*. "Thomas Nast has been our best recruiting sergeant," he wrote to the magazine near the end of the war. "His emblematic cartoons have never failed to arouse enthusiasm and patriotism, and have always seemed to come just when these articles were getting scarce."

General Grant was also an admirer of Nast's pictures. "Who is the foremost figure in civil life developed by the Rebellion?" he replied to an interviewer toward the end of the war. "*I think, Thomas Nast. He did as much as any one man to preserve the Union and bring the war to an end.*"

"He did as much as any one man to preserve the Union and bring the war to an end."

On April 9, 1865, Confederate General Robert E. Lee surrendered to Grant in Appomattox, a tiny southern Virginia town, a few miles east of Lynchburg. After four years, the war was finally over. The tragedy and violence had not ended yet, however. On the evening of April 14, President Lincoln was shot and killed by John Wilkes Booth. In response to Lincoln's death, Nast submitted to *Harper's Weekly* his saddest and most moving portraits of the costs of the war: "Victory and Death" and "Columbia Mourns." In the latter picture, Columbia, the normally proud symbol of liberty, has collapsed in tears before Lincoln's casket. In the background, the figures of two soldiers, an infantryman and a sailor, kneel and weep.

CHAPTER FOUR

BOSS TWEED

After Lincoln's death, Nast abandoned the inspir-
ing, sentimental portraits that had made him
famous during the war in favor of a more sarcas-
tic and confrontational style of drawing. Nast's
new technique was known as caricature. It
involved exaggerating the traits or physical fea-
tures of an individual to achieve a sentimental or
comic effect. Sometimes, Nast's caricatures simply made an individual more recognizable to the
viewer. For instance, readers everywhere could
recognize a drawing of Abraham Lincoln at a
glance, simply by the enormous height of the late
president's stovepipe hat. At times, Nast drew
his caricatures with obvious affection, in a way
that endeared the individual to the reader. During
this period, the artist often pictured himself as
frumpy and overweight, creating the image of
someone too consumed with his work to worry
about his appearance.

More often than not, however, Nast's drawings were meant to humiliate and embarrass the people they portrayed. One of the first public figures to suffer the ridicule of Nast's pencil was fellow New Yorker Horatio Seymour. A Democrat who had opposed Lincoln's war policies, Seymour was chosen by his party to run against Ulysses S. Grant in the presidential election of 1868. In his coverage of the election for *Harper's,* Nast consistently portrayed Grant as a war hero in his Union uniform. Seymour, on the other hand, was pictured as a devilish figure. The Democratic candidate was almost completely bald, with a large tuft of white hair above each ear. In his drawings, Nast turned these tufts of hair into full devils' horns and depicted Seymour in a series of villainous roles, including Lady Macbeth and the serpent in the Garden of Eden.

The drawings had a devastating impact on the attitudes of readers—and voters—toward the Democratic candidate. Grant won the election by a large margin and gave Nast a great share of the credit for his victory. "Two things elected me," he would later write, "the sword of Sheridan and the pencil of Thomas Nast."

THE TWEED RING

Nast's most important work during this period would be reserved for William Marcy "Boss"

Tweed and the other members of the infamous Tweed Ring, who controlled New York City politics. In a little more than 15 years, Tweed had risen from the Greenwich Village fire chief of Nast's youth to the most powerful man in New York. He had not earned his position honestly, however.

Since the end of the Civil War, Boss Tweed—as he was known by his friends and enemies alike—had assembled the most corrupt group of political opportunists in U.S. history. Tweed's partners in crime included the most prominent figures in city and state government. "Elegant" Abraham Oakey Hall was the mayor of New York. Richard "Slippery Dick" Connolly was the city comptroller. Peter "Brains" Sweeney served as both city treasurer and the president of the Department of Public Parks. John Hoffman was governor. Tweed himself served in several important state and municipal government positions. He was president of the city legislature's board of supervisors, commissioner of public works, deputy street commissioner, and state senator.

Together, Tweed and his partners controlled virtually every aspect of political and economic life in the city. Their headquarters at the time was a popular New York City political organization known as Tammany Hall. The Society of Tammany, as it had originally been called, was founded in 1779 as a social and patriotic club. By the 1860s, its members controlled almost all the city's important political offices.

During the five years they ruled New York, the Tweed Ring used their power and influence to steal millions of dollars from the city. One of their favorite activities was to award phony contracts to their friends and associates for buildings and roads that were never constructed and services that were never provided. In each case, Tweed and his cohorts kept a healthy percentage of the money for themselves. The Tweed Ring also paid themselves and their friends enormous salaries for the work that they actually did perform.

Few things angered Nast more than the use of privilege and power to take advantage of others, so it's not surprising that he decided to use his drawing pencils to expose the Tweed Ring to the public. From 1870 to 1871, the artist produced several of his most powerful drawings for *Harper's* in a relentless assault on the Tweed Ring's corruption and greed.

In what was perhaps his most famous drawing of all, Nast portrayed a ferocious tiger poised proudly at the center of a huge coliseum. While an enormous crowd watches from the grandstands, the tiger stands over slaughtered Columbia, the robed symbol of American liberty, and growls defiantly at the viewer. Beneath the drawing, Nast challenged the reader with the words: "What are you going to do about it."

Nast borrowed the face of the tiger from the emblem on the fire truck at Tweed's old Big Six Fire Company in lower Manhattan. The artist had feared and admired the image as a child, and now he used it as a symbol of the savagery and greed of the Tweed Ring. For millions of Americans, the "Tammany Tiger" would become the most enduring image of the Tweed scandal.

Nast was joined in his assault on the Tweed Ring by Louis Jennings, the newly hired editor of the *New York Times*. An English journalist who loved a good fight, Jennings regularly wrote scathing editorials condemning the corruption of the city government.

Tweed and his associates had accumulated so much money and power, however, that they appeared to be above both the law and the influence of the press. Throughout the city, the most powerful people were on their payrolls. Whenever one of their members was threatened with exposure, they always found a way to elude their investigators. They bribed judges and jurors, paid off auditors and police officers, and blackmailed political opponents.

They also used money and threats to silence the press. *New York Times* publisher George Jones later claimed to have been offered the sum of $5 million by one of Tweed's representatives to stop his paper's attacks on the city government. During the height of the scandal, Nast himself was offered $500,000 to study painting in Europe by one of Tweed's men. "Well, I don't think I'll do it," he informed the man who made the offer. "I made up my mind not long ago to put some of those fellows behind bars, and I'm going to put them there."

As far as Tweed was concerned, the payment of half a million dollars to silence Nast would have been a bargain. Tweed once confessed that he feared the artist and his drawings even more than Jennings's powerful editorials for the *New York Times*. "I don't give a straw for your newspaper articles," he told a reporter. "My constituents don't know how to read, but they can't help seeing them damned pictures."

> **"My constituents don't know how to read, but they can't help seeing them damned pictures."**

Things began to fall apart for Boss Tweed and his partners on January 21, 1871, when county auditor James Watson was killed in a freak sleighing accident. Watson had played an important role in maintaining the Ring's financial records and keeping their illegal activities hidden from the public. He was quickly replaced by a young man named Matthew O'Rourke. Unknown to the Tweed Ring, one of its members had refused to honor a claim that O'Rourke had made against the city a few years earlier. O'Rourke still held a bitter grudge and decided to get even. As soon as he took office and gained access to the city's records, he copied figures documenting the Ring's corrupt financial dealings and sent them straight to Jennings at the *New York Times.*

While O'Rourke was scouring through the Tweed Ring's financial records, former sheriff Jimmy O'Brien was devising his own plot to expose the Ring. O'Brien had recently been involved in a political movement known as the New Democracy, which struggled to defeat Tweed and his corrupt political associates. Like O'Rourke, he had also been cheated out of money by the Tweed Ring in the past. When the New Democracy movement failed to unseat the current city government, O'Brien decided to take matters into his own hands. With the help of his friend William Copeland, who secured a job in the city comptroller's office, O'Brien managed to smuggle out city records documenting the illegal activities of Tweed and his partners. Following O'Rourke's example, O'Brien and Copeland also sent their information straight to the *New York Times.*

Finally, Jennings and Nast had actual facts and figures to prove their charges that the Tweed

Ring was corrupt. Armed with the new evidence, both the *New York Times* and *Harper's Weekly* now became even more aggressive in their attacks on the city government. During the next few months, the pages of *Harper's* featured some of the harshest and most powerful caricatures of Nast's career. In the most damaging portrait, Tweed and his cohorts were pictured standing in a circle. Each one of them was shown pointing a finger at one of the other members of the Ring in response to the caption: "Who stole the people's money?"

With public opinion against them and several official investigations now underway, the members of the Tweed Ring were finally driven from office during the elections of November 1871. Peter Sweeney and Richard Connolly both fled the country immediately, before they were brought to trial for their crimes. Mayor Oakey Hall was forced from office but never served a day in prison. He was tried three times for separate crimes but was acquitted on each occasion because of a technicality.

For some reason, Boss Tweed decided not to run away. He was tried and convicted for fraud in 1873 and sentenced to 12 years in federal prison. Tweed still had powerful friends in the courts and on the prison boards, however, and he was released after serving little more than a year of his sentence. But even a year in prison had been too much for Tweed. After he was indicted on new charges in 1875, Tweed followed Connolly and Sweeney's example and fled the country for Cuba.

Ironically, it would be one of Nast's drawings for *Harper's Weekly* that would finally lead to Tweed's capture and arrest. In the days following his escape, U.S. authorities searched throughout Cuba for the former political boss. Informed that he had recently sailed for Spain, they wired the Spanish police that an escaped American criminal would soon be attempting to enter their country. The Spanish police had never seen Tweed, however, and no one in Cuba had an actual photograph to send them. Instead, they sent one of Nast's caricatures from a recent issue of *Harper's Weekly*.

Tweed arrived in Spain disguised as an American sailor. With the help of the Nast drawing, however, the Spanish police were easily able to recognize him. He was immediately arrested and sent back to the United States to face trial. On the return journey across the Atlantic Ocean, his bags were searched by the U.S. authorities. To their surprise, they discovered that one of them was filled with Nast's caricatures of the Tweed Ring, including the drawing that had led to Tweed's arrest. Less than two years later, Boss Tweed died in the midst of an ongoing investigation of the Tweed Ring's illegal activities.

A THOMAS NAST SAMPLER

THIS NAST SELF-PORTRAIT APPEARED ON THE FRONT PAGE
OF THE JULY 19, 1879, ISSUE OF *HARPER'S WEEKLY*.

In this cartoon, Nast caricatures Senator Carl Schurz. Nast's political caricatures were a popular feature in *Harper's Weekly* and other publications.

IN THIS CARTOON PUBLISHED DURING THE 1872
PRESIDENTIAL CAMPAIGN, NAST RIDICULES THE ATTEMPT
BY THE DEMOCRATS TO ELECT HORACE GREELEY,
PICTURED HERE AS A TROJAN HORSE. THE CAPTION READ,
"ANYTHING TO GET IN."

In this drawing, Nast portrays William "Boss" Tweed
and his cohorts in the Tweed Ring, as vultures on the
edge of a cliff. They appear to be waiting for scandal
to blow over so they could resume their plundering
of New York City's resources. The Caption read, "A
Group of Vultures Waiting for the Storm to "Blow
Over."—'Let Us *Prey*.'"

NAST SHOWS FOUR TAMMANY HALL CONSPIRATORS HIDING
IN A BASEMENT AS THE SHADOWS OF FOUR HANGMAN'S
NOOSES HOVER ON THE WALL ABOVE THEIR HEADS. THE
CAPTION READ, "THE ONLY THING THEY RESPECT OR FEAR."

NAST'S ILLUSTRATIONS OF THE CIVIL WAR HELPED
SUSTAIN PUBLIC SUPPORT FOR LINCOLN'S WAR EFFORTS.
THIS DRAWING APPEARED IN A NOVEMBER 1863
ISSUE OF *HARPER'S WEEKLY*.

NAST POPULARIZED THE IMAGE OF THE ELEPHANT AS THE
SYMBOL OF THE REPUBLICAN PARTY AND THE DONKEY AS
THE SYMBOL THE DEMOCRATIC PARTY. THIS IS THE FIRST
DRAWING IN WHICH THE SYMBOLS APPEARED TOGETHER.

THIS ILLUSTRATION SHOWS THE REPUBLICAN VIEW OF THE DEMOCRATIC PARTY'S ATTACK ON THE RECONSTRUCTION ACTS, WHICH PROTECTED AFRICAN-AMERICANS.

IN THIS DRAWING, NAST DRAWS ATTENTION TO
THE ATTEMPTS BY WHITE SOUTHERNS TO INTIMATE
AND CONTROL BLACKS IN THE SOUTH.

NAST SUPPORTED THE RIGHTS OF MINORITIES.
THE CARTOON ABOVE TAKES AIM AT THE 1884 LAW
THAT BANNED CHINESE IMMIGRATION INTO THE UNITED
STATES. THE CARTOON ON THE LEFT ASKS WHETHER THE
BLACK SOLDIERS WHO FOUGHT FOR THE UNION SHOULD
BE ALLOWED THE RIGHT TO VOTE. THE CAPTION READ,
"FRANCHISE AND NOT THIS MAN?"

NAST DREW THIS ILLUSTRATION AS A REMEMBRANCE OF PRES-
IDENT JAMES A. GARFIELD, WHO DIED ON SEPTEMBER 19,
1881, FROM THE WOUNDS INFLICTED BY AN ASSASSIN.

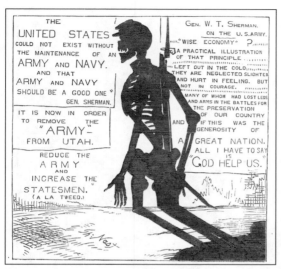

N<small>AST</small>'S <small>ILLUSTRATIONS COVERED A VARIETY OF SOCIAL AND</small>
<small>POLITICAL ISSUES, FROM WHETHER THE SIZE OF THE ARMY</small>
<small>SHOULD BE SHRUNK</small> (<small>TOP</small>) <small>TO ECONOMIC ISSUES</small> (<small>BOTTOM</small>).

Nast popularized the image of
Santa Claus. His first Santa Claus drawing,
Santa in Camp (above) appeared in 1863,
and one of his most popular Santa Claus
illustrations (right) showed the jolly elf
reading letters from children.

NAST POKES FUN AT HIMSELF
IN THIS SELF-PORTRAIT.

CHAPTER FIVE

THE PRINCE OF POLITICAL CARTOONISTS

After the defeat of the Tweed Ring in the 1871 elections, Nast discovered that he had suddenly become a national celebrity. To many Americans, he was as admired and respected as the politicians, military leaders, and other public figures he celebrated in his cartoons.

One of Nast's biggest admirers was President Ulysses S. Grant. In the past, Grant had given the artist a large part of the credit for both the Union's victory in the Civil War and his own successful candidacy for president. Now planning to run for a second term as president, Grant was eager to secure the support of Nast and his drawing pencils.

On a visit to Washington, D.C., in February 1872, Nast was greeted by the president as if he were a visiting dignitary or a military hero returning home from the war. Dinners and banquets were held in his honor by various government officials, and he was invited to attend special meetings of Grant's cabinet. Even some of Nast's political enemies went out of their way to treat the artist with courtesy and respect.

"It certainly is funny," Nast wrote home to his wife Sarah during the visit, "how all the senators are in a flutter about my being here, and are all afraid that I will do them up [draw caricatures of them]. . . . The power I have here frightens me."

"The power I have here frightens me."

Horace Greeley was chosen as the Democratic candidate for president at the party's national convention in July 1872. The beloved newspaper editor for the *New York Tribune* was an easy target for Nast's humorous drawings. Greeley was frequently moved by his emotional response to an issue, and he often changed his position on an issue several times. Throughout the campaign, Nast was able to use Greeley's past reputation as an editor and journalist against him. For the most part, Nast portrayed the Democratic candidate not as evil, but as foolish, overemotional, and inconsistent in his beliefs and opinions.

Curiously, Nast himself actually became an object of cartoon caricature during the final days of the campaign. Nast's friend and fellow political cartoonist, Frank Bellew, had recently been hired as an illustrator by the *Fifth Avenue Journal*. The *Journal* was a rival of *Harper's Weekly* and a fervent supporter of Greeley's candidacy for president. Bellew's cartoons portrayed Nast as a ruthless opportunist who would stop at nothing to win the election for Grant. One illustration showed the artist standing eagerly beside an enormous bowl of mud. The caption read: "Mixing Day at Harper's—Making Mud to Fling at Greeley." For his part, Nast proved to have a much better sense of humor than many of his political opponents. In spite of the satirical cartoons, he and Bellew remained close friends throughout the campaign.

With the support of Nast and the rest of the staff at *Harper's Weekly*, Grant won the election by a large margin. The campaign had been particularly hard on Greeley. His wife had died after a long battle with tuberculosis shortly before the election. His friends reported that he had also been deeply hurt by some of Nast's cartoons, particularly those suggesting that he had been dishonest. Less than a month after the election, on November 29, 1872, Greeley died suddenly at the age of 61.

Once again, Nast was praised by President Grant and a host of other notable figures for his role in the election. One of the most impressive tributes came from the great American humorist Mark Twain, the author of *Roughing It* and *The Adventures of Huckleberry Finn*.

Twain wrote:

Nast, you more than any other man have won a prodigious victory for Grant—I mean, rather, for Civilization and Progress. Those pictures were simply marvelous, and if any man in the land has a right to hold his head up and be honestly proud of his share in this year's vast events, that man is unquestionably yourself. We all do sincerely honor you and are proud of you.

All the words of praise suddenly seemed hollow to Nast, however. For one thing, he felt guilty and depressed for the role that he felt he had played in Greeley's illness and death. Now 32 years old, he was also exhausted by his nonstop schedule during the days of the campaign. At the end of the year, he took a leave of absence from *Harper's Weekly* and embarked on a lecture tour of England and the United States. For almost five months, he did not publish a single political cartoon. Nast missed the excitement and controversy of political cartooning, however, and he was soon back at work at *Harper's Weekly*.

THE ELEPHANT

During the congressional elections of 1874, many Republican candidates sought votes by adopting popular Democratic positions on issues like inflation and the reduction of the military. Although these positions were popular at the time, Nast still believed that they were bad for the nation. He felt that Republicans who adopted these positions might gain a few votes in the current election, but they would ultimately weaken both their party and the nation.

To express this fear, Nast drew a cartoon in which a huge elephant was pursued by a group of smaller wild animals. The elephant did not notice that it was about to tumble into the edge of a deep pit. For Nast, the elephant in the picture symbolized the Republican candidates and voters. The other wild animals represented the popular Democratic positions that were forcing them toward political ruin. For the rest of his career, Nast would use the elephant to represent the Republican Party. Eventually, the animal would be adopted by the party as its official symbol, a symbol that is still used today.

THE 1876 ELECTION

As Grant had repeatedly promised in his previous campaign, he did not run for a third term in 1876. In his place, the Republicans chose Ohio governor Rutherford B. Hayes. He was opposed in the election campaign by Samuel J. Tilden, a popular Democratic governor of New York. Tilden had recently played a major role in defeating the Tweed Ring. Both men were proven leaders and strong candidates. Even with Nast and *Harper's Weekly* lending their support to the Hayes campaign, the election proved to be one of the closest in U.S. history.

When the electoral votes were counted, Hayes was declared the winner by a narrow margin. Tilden's supporters protested the results, however, claiming that the votes had been miscounted in several Southern states. An agreement was reached through which each party sent its own representatives to the states in question to supervise the recounting of the votes. Once again, Hayes was declared the victor—this time by an even narrower margin.

CHAPTER SIX

TROUBLE AT HARPER'S WEEKLY

In the spring of 1877, Nast received a crushing blow to both his personal and his professional life. Fletcher Harper, the artist's publisher at *Harper's Weekly,* died suddenly and unexpectedly.

For more than 15 years, Harper had been Nast's mentor and his friend. From the beginning of Nast's career at *Harper's Weekly,* the fair-minded publisher had given the young artist the freedom and support to develop into the most accomplished and respected political cartoonist of his age. On numerous occasions, Harper had also protected Nast from the criticism and censorship of the magazine's editor, George William Curtis. Over the years, Curtis and Nast had often disagreed on the issues. Even when they had shared the same opinions, Curtis sometimes felt that Nast's caricatures were too harsh or controversial.

Nast resented the idea that the opinions

expressed in his cartoons for *Harper's Weekly* should be in any way affected by his editor's personal political beliefs. Although Curtis regularly complained about Nast's controversial cartoons, the artist consistently refused to remove the drawings or change them to make them less offensive. "I only draw what I believe to be right," he explained to Curtis on another occasion. "I do not wish to recall it."

Throughout the private conflict between Curtis and Nast, Fletcher Harper had continued to support the work of his gifted young artist. "There is a great pressure against me for making fun of [Republican senators] Schurz, Sumner, etc.," Nast wrote to his wife at the time, "but I hear that the Harpers will stand by me, no matter what happens." For Fletcher Harper, the magazine's strength was in its willingness to present a variety of political opinions. *Harper's Weekly,* he felt, was big enough for the opinions of both Thomas Nast and George William Curtis—even when the two men disagreed. As long as Harper remained publisher, Nast was given free reign to express himself through his drawings, no matter how controversial they were.

Things began to change at *Harper's Weekly* after Fletcher Harper's death, however. His successor as publisher, his nephew J. W. "Joe Brooklyn" Harper, Jr., was also a capable newsman and

Harper's Weekly *publisher Fletcher Harper always gave Nast freedom to express his opinions.*

a longtime admirer of Nast's work. Joe Harper was more timid than his uncle when controversy was involved, however, and he tended to support William Curtis's desire for a "party line" in the magazine's general editorial policy. Curtis did not approve of publishing anything that did not support the Republican Party and its positions on the issues.

In spite of this, Nast did produce several strong illustrations during the early years of Joe Harper's management of the magazine, including a few that were critical of the Republican administration. Some of the artist's more aggressive and colorful drawings were in response to President Hayes's Southern policy.

After the Civil War ended, federal troops were sent to occupy the South, both to prevent further armed rebellions and to ensure that the rights of freed slaves were observed by the white majority. Now that 10 years had passed, the majority of Americans felt that these troops should finally be removed. Nast and many other Republicans feared that the removal of troops would be disastrous for African-Americans, however, especially at election time. In recent years, secret organizations, such as the Ku Klux Klan, had been formed in the South to harass and intimidate newly freed slaves. Without soldiers to guard the election booths, Nast argued, many Southern blacks would be too frightened to exercise their right to vote. This would mean that white Democrats would unfairly regain control of local and state governments in the South.

Tens of thousands of Union soldiers had given their lives to free the slaves and establish their full rights as U.S. citizens. Nast was determined to do his part to ensure that their rights were preserved in the years following the war. On September 5, 1868, his powerful illustration, "This Is a White Man's Government," had been published in *Harper's Weekly*. In the drawing, a group of white men stood on the back of a black Union soldier. The group included a Northern businessman, a Democratic politician, and a Confederate war veteran. While the three men laughed and talked together, the black man at their heels still clung defiantly to the Union flag.

President Hayes disagreed with Nast's picture of life in the post-Civil War South. Under pressure from the Democratic Party and Southern voters, he began to remove federal troops from many Southern cities and towns, initiating a policy that gave much greater control to the white Southern majority.

THE 1880 ELECTION

Management at *Harper's Weekly* became less tolerant of Nast's dissenting opinions during the 1880 presidential election, however. The Republican party chose James A. Garfield, the former general and congressman from Ohio. In spite of his desire for a Republican victory, Nast had serious misgivings about Garfield's qualifications as a presidential candidate. A few years earlier, Garfield had been involved in a serious political scandal involving the Union Pacific Railroad.

For Nast, the whole episode reeked of the

same type of greed and corruption that he had campaigned against in the Tweed Ring affair. Against the protest of his editor, George William Curtis, he produced a drawing condemning the activities of the congressmen who had been accused of corruption. A few months after the controversy, Nast and Garfield were introduced at a gathering in Washington, and Nast refused to shake the former general's hand. "I know why you will not shake hands with me," Garfield had declared angrily at the time. "That will all be explained some day."

At the time of Garfield's nomination in 1880, the matter had still not been explained to Nast's satisfaction, however. Although Nast agreed not to ridicule Garfield in his drawings, he also refused to endorse the Republican candidate. For the most part, his cartoons during the campaign focused on the issues. There were numerous drawings of proud Republican elephants and angry Democratic tigers. What was missing were the powerful personal caricatures that had been Nast's hallmark in the past.

The greatest conflict between Nast and *Harper's Weekly* occurred over the nomination of General Winfield S. Hancock as the candidate chosen by the Democrats to oppose Garfield. Hancock was a former Civil War hero, and Nast regarded him as a person of unquestionable integrity. The candidate and the political cartoonist were also close friends. In the early days of the campaign, Nast refused to draw cartoons ridiculing Hancock.

At first, Nast and the magazine reached a compromise on the artist's treatment of the two presidential candidates. Nast would stick strictly to the issues in his cartoons and for the most part leave both men out of his drawings. In order to satisfy their Republican readers, the magazine would hire a team of young artists to provide the humorous, pro-Republican caricatures they expected to see from Nast.

This arrangement managed to satisfy both Nast and the magazine's readers for several weeks. Late in the summer, however, Nast submitted a cartoon that portrayed Hancock in his Union uniform as a gallant and brave Civil War hero. Claiming that Nast had rejected his end of the bargain, *Harper's Weekly* refused to publish the drawing. Nast was furious and threatened to leave the magazine. Eventually, Curtis persuaded him to return. It had become clear to the artist, however, that he would never again enjoy the freedom and support that he had received from Fletcher Harper.

As it turned out, Nast soon found plenty of things to ridicule in Hancock. While he may have been a commanding figure on the battlefield, he proved to be completely incompetent when it came to campaign politics. The Democratic candidate appeared to have little grasp or knowledge of the day's important issues and often refused to respond to questions from the press. As much as Nast admired Hancock's achievements during the war, the artist could not overlook the general's weakness as a presidential candidate, nor could he ignore his responsibility to expose Hancock's political shortcomings to the magazine's readers. When the votes were counted in November, Garfield had triumphed over Hancock by a narrow margin—214 electoral votes for the Republican candidate to 155 for the Democrat.

THE MUGWUMP REVOLT

On July 2, 1881, President Garfield was shot by a disgruntled Republican office seeker. For almost two months, the wounded president lay in a hospital bed on the verge of death. As the nation prayed for Garfield's recovery, Nast produced a double-paged drawing entitled, "God Save the President" for *Harper's Weekly*. When Garfield finally died, on September 19, Nast drew one of his most moving illustrations, entitled "After All." In the drawing, a grief-stricken Columbia has collapsed before an altar with her head in her arms. "Though love and life make tearful intercession," proclaimed the poem in the picture's caption, "death cometh after all." Immediately after his death, Garfield was replaced as president by Vice President Chester A. Arthur.

Nast was becoming increasingly dissatisfied with his role at *Harper's Weekly,* however. His drawings were now frequently rejected or delayed by the magazine's editors. The rejections were partially a result of a change in printing technique. Throughout the early years of Nast's career, artists who worked in such print media as magazines and newspapers were able to reproduce their work through a system known as hand engraving. Hand engravers used soft pencils to etch their designs into the smooth, hard surface of a boxwood block. Illustrations were then printed directly from the ink-soaked block onto the page. Over the years, Nast had matured into the undisputed master of this technique.

In the 1870s, however, a new print technique, known as process or photochemical reproduction, had begun to replace the old hand-engraved method. Process reproduction used photographed images to reproduce an illustration drawn on paper. Significantly for newspaper and magazine illustrators, the new reproduction technique required the use of pen and ink in drawing, a method that Nast had rarely used in the past. Consequently, several of his first attempts in the new style were clumsier and less accomplished than his normal work. At first, Nast accepted the fact that his inexperience with the new method accounted for some of the *Harper*'s editors' problems with his recent work.

Nast, however, was a proud man and an accomplished artist, and he soon adjusted to the demands of the new printing technique. When several of his drawings were still rejected by the editors at *Harper's Weekly,* Nast sent an angry letter to the magazine's acting publisher, John W. Harper, threatening to resign:

> Since you have taken exclusive charge of my drawings, they have appeared less and less frequently in the Weekly, and I think I have observed faithfully the letter of the agreement. For some years my past work has been refused at times, but some reason has been assigned to it, generally that the subjects were adverse to the interests of the house.
>
> Of late, however, no such motive could apply, for noticing how often they were suppressed I have been careful to avoid doubtful subjects. Still they have met the same fate persistently, and whenever you have selected any for publication you have invariably chosen the smallest.
>
> Hence, I am forced to the conclusion that

for some reason unknown to me, my drawings are no longer of use to you, and that under the circumstances you certainly cannot care to continue the arrangements with me.

Harper and his colleagues at *Harper's Weekly* may have disagreed with some of Nast's positions on the issues, but they were clearly aware of the illustrator's importance to the magazine. Nast's drawings consistently received more letters of appreciation than any other feature. And whenever one of his drawings did not appear for one or more issues, readers from around the nation wrote the magazine to complain or question his whereabouts. With this in mind, Harper persuaded Nast to stay with *Harper's Weekly,* ensuring the illustrator that more of his drawings would be included in future issues.

Nast was serious about his threats to leave *Harper's Weekly,* however. Now in his early forties, he was the most admired and respected political cartoonist in the nation, and he knew that he could easily get work from the magazine's competitors whenever he wanted it.

During the previous decade, Nast had also become a very wealthy man. Drawing was something that he now did for pleasure and out of his passionate commitment to American politics—not something that he had to do in order to make a living. Increasingly, he found himself taking time off from the magazine to travel abroad and spend time at home with his family and friends.

Early in 1884, Nast was shocked to learn he had lost $30,000 in an investment that he had made the year before. The loss meant that he could no longer enjoy the freedom to which he had grown accustomed in recent years. Once again, he became a working artist, faced with meeting deadlines and satisfying editors' demands in order to make a living.

The 1884 presidential election gave rise to a controversy that reunited Nast with the editors and publishers at *Harper's Weekly*. After a bitterly fought battle at the Republican National Convention, Maine Senator James G. Blaine was chosen over President Chester A. Arthur to head his party's presidential ticket. In the past, Nast had frequently ridiculed Blaine in his drawings. He opposed the senator both for his involvement in the Union Pacific Railroad scandal of 1873 and for his positions on such issues as tariff regulation and civil service reform.

Following the nomination, Nast informed John Harper and George William Curtis that he refused to support the Republican candidate in his drawings for the magazine. "Speaking for myself," he said, "I positively decline to support

Blaine, either directly or indirectly, even if the Democrats should nominate the Devil himself." For once, the two men agreed with his position. Branding themselves as Independents, Nast and the rest of the staff at *Harper's Weekly* joined together with the *New York Times* and other prominent Republicans to support the Democratic nominee for president, New York Governor Grover Cleveland. Suddenly, the artist found himself a leading figure in the Democratic candidate's presidential campaign.

Predictably, Nast and his fellow Independents were widely ridiculed by those Republicans who remained loyal to the party. Nicknamed the Mugwumps, they were criticized in newspaper editorials, vilified in poetry and songs, and caricatured in the political cartoons of pro-Republican magazines. "Tom Nast, the libelous caricaturist, has become a drunken sot and a bar-room loafer," wrote the editor of a Pennsylvania newspaper. A writer for another popular magazine set his contempt for the artist to verse:

Poor, poor T. Nast,
Thy day is past—
Thy bolt is shot, thy die is cast—
Thy pencil point
Is out of joint—
Thy pictures lately disappoint.

A cartoon by the artist A. R. Waud depicted Nast as a collaborator with the ghost of Boss William Tweed. "Go right along," Tweed said in the caption, encouraging Nast's support for the Democratic candidate. "You are now arrayed against my old enemy, the Republican Party."

Nast refused to be intimidated by any of these harsh words and images. In fact, he seemed to thrive in the renewed spirit of colorful caricatures and personal attacks that had been so common in political campaigns only a decade earlier. When the votes were counted in November, Cleveland won the election by one of the narrowest margins in history. The Democratic candidate carried the state of New York by only 1,047 votes. It was the first time in 28 years that a Democrat had been elected president.

CHAPTER SEVEN

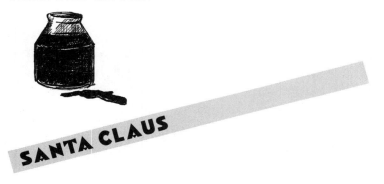

Political cartoons were not the only source of Nast's fame during the late nineteenth century. To tens of thousands of boys and girls throughout America, the artist was known not as a great political caricaturist and social crusader but as the creator of the modern image of Santa Claus.

For more than 20 years, the special Christmas issue of *Harper's Weekly* featured a large, double-page illustration by Nast of the fat, jolly, red-suited holiday elf. These drawings originated many of the popular notions about Santa Claus that children and adults still hold today. In one illustration, Santa is pictured on a rooftop, with a huge bag of toys draped across his shoulders, only moments before he squeezes down the chimney. In another, he sits in the back of his workshop, contentedly smoking a pipe while he surveys the work of his elves. Still another drawing shows him walking quietly on his tiptoes, creeping past the bed of two sleeping children on Christmas Eve.

In the early years, Nast also experimented with some other imaginative settings for the Santa Claus story that have not survived as part of the popular imagination. For the 1863 Christmas issue of *Harper's Weekly,* the artist submitted an illustration called "Santa Claus in Camp." It was his first drawing of Santa Claus to appear in the pages of the magazine. Drawn during the height of the Civil War, the illustration presented Santa Claus dressed in an outfit covered with stars and stripes borrowed from the American flag. From the bag on his shoulder, he busily distributes Christmas gifts to the Union soldiers at an isolated military camp. In all Nast's future Christmas illustrations, Santa would wear only the dark wool suit he is pictured in today, and his presents would be strictly reserved for children.

Perhaps the most famous Christmas illustration by Nast was included in the 1866 Christmas issue of *Harper's Weekly.* The huge, double-page drawing portrayed Santa at various stages of his work. At the center, the jolly holiday elf was shown in his workshop, busily knitting a pair of Christmas stockings. To the right, he studies the pages of an enormous book. The book listed the names of those children who had been good during the year and those who had been bad. To the left, he peers through the lens of a telescope to observe children's behavior for himself. The icicles hanging above his head revealed that he was watching from his home at the North Pole. In a picture at the bottom of the page, he climbs a ladder to the top of the house of one lucky child on Christmas Eve.

Nast's final Christmas illustration for *Harper's Weekly* paired his artwork and the famous words of poet Clement Moore. In the picture, two mice were shown snuggled under blankets, fast asleep. Their tiny beds rest between shelved books in the middle of a fireplace mantel. Above them hangs a framed portrait of a smiling, ruddy-cheeked Santa Claus. The caption beneath the illustration contained the now familiar words: "'Twas the night before Christmas, when all through the house, not a creature was stirring, not even a mouse."

Toward the end of his life, Nast revealed to his biographer, Albert Paine, that he borrowed his image of Santa Claus from stories he had learned during his childhood in Landau, Germany. Each Christmas season, German children heard tales about a kind old saint named Pelze-Nicol (Saint Nicholas). On Christmas Eve, Nast explained, Pelze-Nicol visited the homes of all the children in each village or city throughout Germany. While families slept, the fat-bellied saint left presents under the mantel or Christmas tree. For children who had behaved properly during the year, he left an assortment of toys, candy, and cakes. For those who had been bad, he left only a handful of ashes and a cluster of switches with which their parents would punish them the following morning.

Like Nast's Santa Claus, Pelze-Nicol wore a heavy wool suit over his huge round frame. His fat cheeks were covered with a thick white beard. On his bald head, he wore a floppy fur hat, and his nose and cheeks were burned red by the harsh winter wind. He usually carried a large bag on his shoulder, stuffed full of gifts.

A POPULAR ARTIST

In addition to the Santa Claus illustrations, Nast also provided drawings for a number of other children's books during his years at *Harper's Weekly*. His action-filled drawings for Daniel Defoe's classic adventure tale *Robinson Crusoe* were extremely popular among both children and their parents. Even more successful were his humorous illustrations for the best-selling children's book *A Domestic Blockade*. The book told the story of two children who rebelled against their mother's strict rules by building a tiny fortress in the family parlor. It was the most popular children's story of the

Nast provided illustrations for many books, including this one for the children's classic Hans Brinker.

day and provided thousands of children with their first exposure to Nast's work.

Nast's popularity during the period extended far beyond his published work in books, magazines, and newspapers. He also made a name for himself by drawing and painting caricatured portraits of local celebrities. The artist's humorous caricatures in *Harper's Weekly* sometimes had a devastating impact on the careers of his political opponents, such as Boss Tweed and Horace Greeley. Outside the realm of politics, however, it increasingly became a symbol of prestige to have been caricatured at the hands of Nast's pencil or brush.

In April 1866, the artist presented his first public exhibition of caricatures. It featured 60 life-size paintings of well-known New Yorkers of the day—from such political leaders as the governor and mayor to various socialites and entertainers. Most of the people portrayed in the exhibition were extremely flattered to have been included, and the show was an enormous success with the public.

Nast's caricatures became so popular during the 1860s and 1870s that two local businessmen, the Anthony brothers, produced a series of postcards from photographs of the paintings at one of the artist's shows. Thousands of these postcards were purchased by tourists during the period and then mailed to friends and relatives around the world.

At the same time that he was drawing political cartoons for *Harper's Weekly,* Nast also submitted caricatures to a number of nonpolitical papers and magazines. These included the magazine's sister publication, *Harper's Bazaar,* and a popular humor-oriented newspaper called *Phunny Phellow.* For the latter publication, Nast chose not to sign his name to his portraits and cartoons. Over time, his anonymous illustrations for *Phunny Phellow* became as popular as his political work for *Harper's Weekly.* Few people recognized that the two bodies of work were drawn by the same hand, however. The *Phunny Phellow* illustrations eventually became so successful, in fact, that Nast received the following warning from a friend who feared that the new illustrator might replace Nast as the most popular cartoonist of the day. "You'll have to look to your laurels, Nast," cautioned the well-meaning friend, "that chap on *Phunny Phellow* is after you."

As Nast's reputation grew throughout America, the artist began to compile his own privately published booklets of illustrations and caricatures. In 1871, he published the first issue of *Nast's Almanac.* Many of the day's most popular comic writers—including Josh Billings, Mark Twain, and Petroleum V. Nasby—contributed

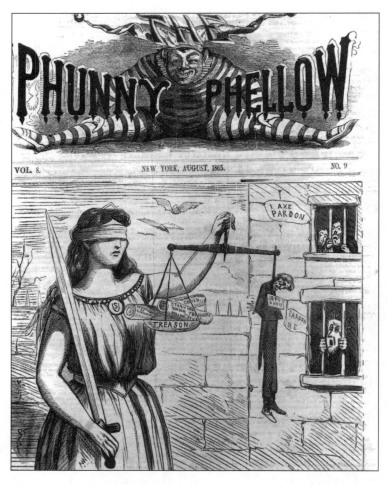

Nast drew this unsigned cover illustration for The Phunny Phellow. *Some of his best friends didn't even recognize Nast's drawings in the humor publication.*

In this drawing, Nast caricatures his good friend Mark Twain.

jokes and funny stories to accompany Nast's humorous drawings. In return, Nast provided caricatures and drawings to illustrate other humorous booklets and almanacs produced by his famous literary friends. Unlike the comic newspapers to which Nast contributed his work during the period, several of these almanacs and booklets were not simply intended for fun, but also addressed important social and political issues. A number of them combined the sharp political satire of *Harper's Weekly* with the good-natured humor of *Phunny Phellow*.

The pairing of Nast and Mark Twain in *Nast's Almanac* gave readers around the country a rare opportunity to see the finest comic writer and the best political cartoonist of the day working together. In their later years, the two men became close friends. They frequently exchanged letters and produced several published works together over the years.

CHAPTER EIGHT

THE FINAL YEARS

The Mugwump Revolt against the Republican Party would be the last time that Nast and his employers at *Harper's Weekly* would see eye to eye on an important political issue.

During the campaign, Nast worked closely with George William Curtis and John Harper to ensure the election of the Democratic candidate. Following the victory, the three men toasted their success and their future together at the magazine. But their good will lasted only briefly. Within a few months, the editors at *Harper's Weekly* were once again either refusing to publish Nast's drawings or sending them back for corrections.

This time, Nast did not respond to the mistreatment from his publishers with angry letters or threats of resignation, however. The artist knew that the quality of many of his drawings had suffered in recent months. The reason, he

In this cartoon, Nast makes fun of the shrinking
demand for his work.

explained to his friends, was that he simply did
not care as much about the issues and personali-
ties that made the newspaper headlines as he had
in the past.

The middle-aged artist missed the days of the

Civil War and the Tweed Ring scandal. In the past, it had been much easier to take sides, to tell who was right and who was wrong on a social or economic issue. Inspired by the certainty of his convictions, Nast had produced the best work of his career: the great Civil War murals, the moving tributes to Lincoln and Grant, the vicious Tammany Hall Tiger, and the slow but reliable Republican elephant. Now his heroes, Lincoln and Garibaldi, were dead, and Grant, bankrupt and humiliated, had been forced into retirement. Instead of great wars and crusades against political corruption, politicians now devoted their speeches to more complicated social and economic issues, such as tariff legislation and civil service reform. It was simply not a situation in which Nast's talents could thrive.

"I cannot do it," he sadly explained to a friend who had expressed concern over the lack of passion in Nast's recent work. "I cannot outrage my convictions."

On July 23, 1885, Nast learned that his old friend, Ulysses S. Grant, had died suddenly. Although the news of the former president's death did not come as a surprise, Nast was overwhelmed with grief. After the deaths of Lincoln and Garibaldi, Grant had been the last remaining hero of his youth. The great general's death seemed to Nast like the end of an era. The two-page drawing that the artist submitted to *Harper's Weekly* to mark Grant's death was one of the saddest and most moving illustrations of his career. It portrayed various scenes from Grant's distinguished military and political career, and bore the somber caption: "The Hero of Our Age—Dead."

PARTING WAYS

After Grant's death, Nast submitted fewer and fewer drawings to *Harper's Weekly*. There was a colorful depiction of Boss Tweed in prison and a splendid holiday illustration of "The Night Before Christmas." By the spring of 1888, he had almost completely stopped submitting his drawings to *Harper's Weekly*. When his contract with the magazine expired that summer, he simply neglected to renew it. Unable to reach the artist directly, John Harper sent a telegraph to his home: "We await your return for consideration of a new contract."

By this time, however, Nast had lost all interest in working for his old employer, and he did not respond to Harper's message. This time, there were no arguments and no disagreements, just a simple parting of the ways. As the 1888 presidential campaign grew nearer, *Harper's Weekly* suddenly found themselves without the services of Thomas Nast for the first time in almost 30 years.

Although neither party realized it at the

time, the break between Nast and *Harper's Weekly* had a devastating effect on both the artist and the magazine. "In quitting *Harper's Weekly,* Nast lost his forum," wrote one of Nast's admirers many years later. "In losing him, *Harper's Weekly* lost its political importance."

NEW CHALLENGES

Although he was now an internationally celebrated figure, Nast could not afford to retire after his departure from *Harper's Weekly.* He had lost much of his savings through making bad investments a few years earlier, and he still needed regular employment in order to pay his bills. After a brief lecture tour of the American West, he began regularly contributing his drawings to several popular American newspapers and magazines, including *Time, Once A Week, Collier's Weekly,* and the *Illustrated American.* The latter newspaper gave the artist the opportunity to contribute some of his most colorful drawings of the period. Like many publications of the day, *Collier's Weekly* had trouble finding enough readers and advertisers to covers its expenses, and it soon disappeared from circulation.

In March 1892, Nast became an editor and contributor to the *New York Gazette.* For the first time in the 52-year-old artist's career, the paper's publishers agreed to give him free rein to express his political opinions, no matter how controversial. Under these improved conditions, Nast gradually began to recover some of the humor and enthusiasm that characterized his earlier work. Unfortunately, the paper was struggling for survival, and the publishers barely had enough money to print each issue.

Nast was tired of moving from one paper to another. With the support of his family, he decided to buy the *New York Gazette*. He put a second mortgage on his house to raise the money for the paper, which was renamed *Nast's Weekly*. The artist also appointed his son, Thomas Nast, Jr., as the publisher. Using his connections in the New York publishing company, Nast quickly extended the newspaper's circulation to more than 100,000 readers.

By founding *Nast's Weekly,* Nast fulfilled a 20-year ambition to own a paper that would feature his drawings and represent his positions on the major issues of the day. "Such a paper would do more good than any church or library or college ever founded," he had often explained to his friends in the past. Sadly, it seemed that the audience for such a paper had already come and gone many years earlier. The majority of readers disagreed with Nast's positions on the issues and found his dramatic style of drawing out of date.

Thomas Nast holds his son, Thomas Nast Jr. As an adult, the younger Nast would join his father in running the short-lived Nast's Weekly.

Nast struggled valiantly to make the paper succeed. *Nast's Weekly* campaigned vigorously on behalf of Republican presidential nominee Benjamin Harrison during the election of 1892. After Harrison's defeat by the Democratic candidate, William McKinley, the paper lost the support of a number of important leaders in the New York Republican Party. In the months that followed, its readership declined with each issue. Finally, in the spring of 1893, Nast decided to use the remainder of his investment to pay off his debts and close the paper. Once again, he found himself looking for work.

A NEW CAREER

After the failure of *Nast's Weekly,* the artist finally began to accept that the majority of newspaper readers were no longer interested in his bold style of political cartooning. In 1877, a new illustrated magazine called *Puck* had opened its offices in New York City. *Puck* introduced a new style of illustration to the public. The magazine's chief political cartoonist, Joseph Keppler, favored a style of illustration and caricature that was more subtle and less politically committed than the emotionally charged cartoons made popular by Nast. Rather than take sides on an issue, *Puck*'s writers and illustrators preferred to observe the political process from a distance. Politicians were rarely portrayed as good people or bad people in the pages of *Puck*. For the most part, political leaders were pictured as celebrities in the magazine, along with entertainers, socialites, and other members of the media.

Instead of despairing over the situation, Nast saw it as an opportunity. At the age of 54, he decided to begin a new career as a painter. Over the years, friends and admirers had tried to commission Nast to paint various personal portraits or scenes of historical events. In the past, he had always been too busy with his work as a political cartoonist to accept any of the offers. Suddenly, he found himself free to begin painting at the precise moment that a number of offers came his way.

The first request came from an old friend, publisher H. H. Kohlsaat, in London. At Kohlsaat's invitation, Nast sailed to London in the fall of 1894 to begin work on a large canvas depicting General Lee's surrender to General Grant at Appomattox. Nast went to work on the painting with a degree of enthusiasm he had not displayed in years. He completed it in time for its official unveiling at the Public Library of Galena, Illinois, on April 9, 1895. The date was the thirtieth anniversary of the scene it portrayed.

Immediately after completing the Appomattox painting, Nast went straight to work on another project. The artist's friend Henry Irving commissioned him to present a painting on the subject of the great English poet and playwright William Shakespeare to be installed at the William Winter Memorial on Staten Island, New York.

In the past, Nast had often used scenes and characters from Shakespeare's plays in his political cartoons for *Harper's Weekly*. For his present assignment, Nast chose a simple scene: a sculpted bust of Shakespeare on a table in the room where the poet was born. From either side, the spirits of Comedy and Tragedy advance to place a crown of laurel on the poet's head. The painting was unveiled on Shakespeare's birthday, April 23, 1896. A few years later, a reproduction of the painting was installed among the treasures at the Shakespeare Memorial at Stratford, England.

In 1899, Nast began work on a third painting. The artist's childhood friend William L. Keese commissioned him to paint a portrait of William E. Burton. Burton was an accomplished character actor who had been popular on the New York stage when the two men were still boys. Keese persuaded Nast to portray Burton in one of his silliest and most memorable roles, the character known as "Toodles." The completed painting was hung on the wall of the Players Club in New York City, where both Keese and Nast were members.

Nast works on an oil painting. At the age of 54, he set out on a new career as a painter.

Nast's was proud of his work as a painter, but he still missed newspaper and magazine work and the regular exposure that it gave him to the public. Few readers seemed interested in what the artist had to offer anymore, and he rarely received assignments from the popular press. Uncommissioned drawings that he tried to sell himself were usually returned with a polite letter of rejection. Nast realized sadly that the public was no longer interested in either his political opinions or the way he expressed them in his drawings. "I feel like a caged animal—so helpless!" he complained to his wife at the time.

With Nast's drawings no longer appearing regularly in the press, rumors began to circulate that the artist had died several years earlier. Some people falsely attributed the occasional drawings that did appear—such as a Christmas illustration for *Leslie's Weekly* during the winter of 1901—to Nast's son, Thomas, Jr. The younger Tom Nast had become a talented draftsman in his own right, and many people believed that he submitted the drawings to keep his father's memory alive.

"What is the use to cry about it?" he told a friend in response to one of the many rumors circulating concerning his death. "The paper is right—I'm dead enough to the public."

A JOB OFFER

In March 1902, Nast received an unexpected offer from President Theodore Roosevelt. The offer came in the form of a letter from Secretary of State John Hay, offering Nast a post as the U.S. consul to Ecuador. "The President would like to put it at your disposition," Hay wrote, "but if you think it too far away and too little amusing for a man with the soul of an artist, please say so frankly, and he will keep you in mind if anything better should turn up: but it is heartbreaking business waiting for the vacancies. Our service is so edifying and preservative that few die and nobody resigns."

Although Nast desperately needed the work, he was reluctant to accept the offer. He had no experience in foreign diplomacy, after all, and knew little about the tiny South American country where he would be stationed. He asked Secretary Hay if any other positions were available, either in England or Germany, where he had a better knowledge of both the language and the culture of the people. Unfortunately, the position in Ecuador was the only one available at the time. Reluctantly, Nast accepted the post and sailed for Ecuador on July 1, 1902.

Nast arrived in Guayaquil, the tiny city

where he was stationed, just in time for a yellow fever epidemic. Most of the people in the area lived in conditions of

"Wild dogs run and ruin the city."

extreme poverty. Nast himself lived for a time without water, and complained of "mice, rats, bats, mosquitoes, fleas, spiders and dirt." "Wild dogs run and ruin the city," he wrote in a letter to his wife, along with a sketch of the vicious animals he was describing.

For almost five months, Nast stayed healthy, somehow avoiding the nausea and high fevers that claimed two to four lives each day. On Monday, December 1, however, he complained to his secretary that he was feeling weak and had decided to spend the day resting in his hammock. On Tuesday, Nast returned to his office with a slight fever. For several days, he tried vainly to fulfill his duties. Each night, he collapsed onto his bed, his fever having risen higher than the night before. By the end of the week, Nast's temperature was so high that he became delirious, and he was diagnosed with a full-scale case of yellow fever. On Saturday night, he lapsed into a coma. The next morning, on Sunday, December 6, he died quietly in the presence of two of his assistants.

At the time of his death, Nast's longtime employer, *Harper's Weekly,* provided the most honest appraisal of Nast's achievement to appear in the press. The magazine's moving tribute proclaimed Nast to be the most powerful and influential political cartoonist in the history of American journalism. The article also acknowledged, however, that the artist, who was only 62 years old at the time of his death, had failed to adjust to the changes that had recently transformed his profession. In the decade and a half prior to his death, he had been completely left behind by the more subtle and less emotional style of illustration and political cartooning popularized by *Puck* and its imitators. "He belongs so much to the past," the article sadly concluded, "that the impression has spread that he is an old man."

THE LEGACY OF THOMAS NAST

By the time of his death, Nast had become a forgotten man. His angry, one-sided approach to political cartooning had been replaced by the gentler, less passionate style of Joseph Keppler and the other artists at *Puck*. And the classic hand-engraving technique that Nast had used to create his most celebrated illustrations had long since given way to the smooth flowing lines of process reproduction.

The sudden decline in Nast's popularity may also have been a result of the overwhelming effectiveness of his powerful drawings during the Civil War, the Tweed scandal, and the highly contested presidential elections of the mid-19th century. In most readers' minds, Nast and his drawings would always be associated with the great crises he dramatized and the scandals he exposed with his pencil. With the nation now enjoying a period of peace and prosperity, readers were no longer interested in an artist committed to fighting corruption and righting political wrongs. According to historians Stephen Hess and Milton Kaplan, "[Nast's] raw, impassioned approach to politics could not be taken by the public in prolonged doses." While Nast was always happiest in the midst of a good political fight, the majority of readers, and political cartoonists, preferred a less dramatic approach to the news.

Within a few years of Nast's death, however, a series of new scandals and crises would once again threaten the security of the nation, and a new generation of socially committed journalists and illustrators would take up Nast's banner. During the early years of World War I, George Bellows and other artists of the Ash Can school drew powerful illustrations in the pages of *The Masses* condemning U.S. imperialism and corporate greed. Throughout the 1960s, the brilliant cartoons of Paul Szep and Pulitzer Prize-winner Patrick Oliphant helped shape Americans' attitudes toward the Civil Rights movement and the Vietnam War. The vicious caricatures of President Richard Nixon by political cartoonist Herblock (Herbert Block) provided many Americans with the most memorable images of the Watergate investigation. More recently, artists as varied as caricaturist David Levine of the *New York Times Book Review,* Gary Trudeau of "Doonesbury" fame, the *New York Times'* Sue Coe, and underground cartoonist Robert Crumb have all followed Nast's example by ridiculing powerful people or exposing greed and corruption in their drawings. For each of these artists, Nast's brilliant caricatures of Boss Tweed and his partners during the Tammany Hall scandal remain the single defining moment in the history of American caricaturing and political cartooning.

Nast's most enduring legacy may be his uncanny ability to create vivid symbols to capture the public imagination. Uncle Sam, the Tammany tiger, the Republican elephant, and the classic figure of the bearded, big-bellied, wool-suited Santa Claus—each of these was either created or popularized by Nast, and all of them have become permanent parts of American popular culture. "Everyone has grown to know them all on sight," explain Stephen Hess and Milton Kaplan. "Since cartoonists strive for simplicity and for ideas unencumbered with labels, they use this cast of

Nast often used this humorous self-portrait as a visual aid during his lectures.

characters and eliminate the need for a program to tell the players from the other." For more than a century, Nast's familiar images have shaped the way we think about and respond to the world around us. For millions of Americans who have never heard the name of Thomas Nast, the continuing power of these symbols remains the final tribute to his greatness as an artist.

1840	Thomas Nast born in Landau, Germany, on September 27
1846	Moves to the United States with his mother and siblings
1850	Thomas's father joins family in New York City
1853	Thomas drops out of school and begins taking drawing lessons
1855	Hired as illustrator by *Leslie's Weekly*
1858	Draws illustrations used in the Swill Milk scandal exposé
1859	Starts submitting his work to *Harper's Weekly*
1860	Accepts assignment to cover the Heenan-Sayers fight in England; travels to Italy to cover Garibaldi and the Italian Revolution

1861	Returns to New York; covers Lincoln's inauguration
1862	Hired as regular contributor by *Harper's Weekly*
1862–65	Draws illustrations and cartoons that shaped public opinion during U.S. Civil War
1863	Nast's first Santa Claus drawing appears in *Harper's Weekly*
1870–71	Nast involved in successful campaign to expose the corruption of the Tweed Ring
1872	Supports Grant's reelection; embarks on lecture tour
1876	Supports Rutherford B. Hayes's election campaign
1880	Refuses to support Republican James A. Garfield for president
1884	Supports Democrat Grover Cleveland for president
1888	Ends relationship with *Harper's Weekly*
1892	Becomes editor of the *New York Gazette;* buys the *Gazette* and renames it *Nast's Weekly*
1893	Shuts down *Nast's Weekly* when it proves unsuccessful
1894	Begins painting career
1902	Accepts position as U.S. consul to

Ecuador; dies in Guayaquil, Ecuador, on December 6

1956   U.S. Embassy places plaque in Landau, Germany, in memory of Nast

A NOTE ON SOURCES

The only complete biography of Thomas Nast to appear to date is Albert Paine's *Thomas Nast: His Period and His Pictures* (1904; reprint, New York: Chelsea House, 1980). Paine's lengthy biography was written and originally published at the turn of the century and was based primarily on the artist's personal recollections to the author. A large-scale, critical modern biography of Nast has not yet appeared. Several excellent collections of Nast's caricatures and illustrations have appeared over the years, including Thomas Nast's *Cartoons and Illustrations* (New York: Dover, 1974) and Morton Keller's *The Art and Politics of Thomas Nast* (New York: Oxford University Press, 1968). The biographical information in these and other recent treatments of Nast work rely heavily on the biographical information provided by Paine.

Several libraries around the country have

excellent collections of *Harper's Weekly, Nast's Almanac,* and other magazines, pamphlets and books illustrated by Nast. The Yale University Library and the mid-Manhattan branch of the New York City Public Library proved to be excellent sources for this biography.

FOR MORE INFORMATION

Books:

Hakim, Joy. *Reconstruction and Reform*. New York: Oxford University Press, 1994.

Levison, Nancy S. *Turn of the Century: Our Nation One Hundred Years Ago* (New York: Lodestar, 1994.

Meltzer, Milton. *Mark Twain: A Writer's Life*. New York: Watts, 1985.

O'Brian, Steven. *Ulysses S. Grant*. New York: Chelsea House, 1991.

Paine, Albert. *Thomas Nast: His Period and His Pictures*. New York: Macmillan, 1904; reprint, New York: Chelsea House, 1980.

Redman, Lynn. *How to Draw Caricatures*. Chicago: Contemporary Books, 1985.

Twain, Mark, and Charles D. Warner. *Gilded Age: A Tale of Today*. New York: NAL-Dutton, 1985.

INTERNET RESOURCES:

Because of the changeable nature of the Internet, sites appear and disappear very quickly. These resources offered useful information on Thomas Nast at the time of publication. Internet addresses must be entered with capital and lowercase letters exactly as they appear.

http://www.yahoo.com
The Yahoo directory of the World Wide Web is an excellent place to find Internet sites on any topic.

http://makcom.com/jfpl/nast.htm
This is the home page of the Thomas Nast Society, which seeks to preserve Nast's legacy.

http://www.buffnet.net/~starmist/hast/ nast.htm
http://www.historybuff.com/library/ refnast.html
These two sites each provide information about Thomas Nast and downloadable Nast illustrations.

INDEX

Page numbers in *italics*
indicate illustrations.

Academy of Design, 17
Arnold, George, 19
Arthur, Chester A., 83, 86

Bellew, Frank, 19, 70
Billings, Josh, 95
Blaine, James G., 86–87
Burton, William E., 108

Civil War, 34–43, *58, 66,* 69,
  90, 101, 107, 114
Cleveland, Grover, 87
Comic Monthly, 22
Connolly, Richard "Slippery
  Dick," 46, 51, 52
Copeland, William, 50
Curtis, George William, 75–
  76, 77, 80, 81, 86, 99

Fifth Avenue Journal, 71
Fredericks, Alfred, 22

Garfield, James A., *64,* 79–
  80, 82–83
Garibaldi, Giuseppe, 16,
  27–29, *29,* 31, 37, 101
Grant, Ulysses S., 40–42, 45,
  69, 71–72, 73, 101–2, 107
Greeley, Horace, *55,* 70–72,
  94

Hall, Abraham Oakey, 46,
  51
Hancock, Winfield S., 80–82
Harper, Fletcher, 39, 75–76,
  77, *77,* 81
Harper, J. W. "Joe Brook-
  lyn," 76–78
Harper, John W., 84, 85, 86,
  99, 102

ABOUT THE AUTHOR

David Shirley is the author of many books for young readers, including The History of Rock and Roll and Everyday I Sing the Blues: The Story of B. B. King. His writings have appeared in Option, Rolling Stone, Spin, Chicago Review, Raygun, and New York Press. He lives in Brooklyn, New York.